JULIE FOUDY

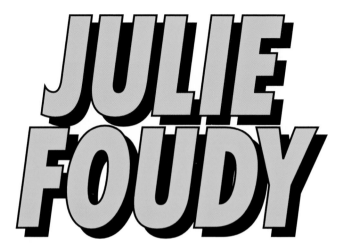

JULIE FOUDY

SOCCER SUPERSTAR

Jeff Savage

Lerner Publications Company • Minneapolis

Library of Congress Cataloging-in-Publication Data

Savage, Jeff, 1961–
    Julie Foudy : soccer superstar / Jeff Savage.
      p. cm.
    Includes bibliographical references (p.) and index.
    Summary: A biography of the young woman from southern California who starred at Stanford University and was a co-captain of the gold medal winning U.S. women's Olympic soccer team in 1996.
    ISBN 0–8225–3662–5 (hardcover : alk. paper).
    ISBN 0–8225–9826–4 (pbk : alk. paper).
    1. Foudy, Julie, 1971–   —Juvenile literature. 2. Soccer players—United States—Biography—Juvenile literature. [1. Foudy, Julie, 1971–   . 2. Soccer players. 3. Women—Biography.]
I. Title.
GV942.7.F63S38   1999
796.334'092—dc21
   [b]   98–30938

Manufactured in the United States of America
1 2 3 4 5 6 – JR – 04 03 02 01 00 99

Contents

Julie and her U.S. teammates found gold in Atlanta.

1

A Golden Goal

Julie Foudy (rhymes with rowdy) tried to ignore the earthquake of stamping feet all around the stadium and the chants of "U-S-A! . . . U-S-A!" She tried to forget how tired she was from running in the warm muggy air, or how her legs ached and her hips throbbed from sliding and lunging for the ball. Julie's team was desperate to score a goal. Just 16 minutes remained in the 1996 Olympic semifinal game, and Team USA trailed Norway, 1–0. The largest crowd ever to watch a women's soccer game in the United States—64,196 people—filled Sanford Stadium in Athens, Georgia. Time was running out in the biggest game of Julie's life. She had to think of a way to help her team score a goal.

Despite two Norwegians **marking** her closely, Julie faked one way and sped off in the other direction to take a pass. She fired a shot toward the goal.

Norway defender Gro Espeseth blocked the ball with her elbow. That's illegal in soccer—except for the **goalkeeper,** who can use her hands and arms—and results in a **penalty kick** for the kicking team. What a great break for Team USA! But referee Sonia Denoncourt did not blow her whistle. She did not call the foul. The Norwegians cleared the ball back down the field. The American players stood shocked.

"You just missed the call!" screamed Julie, running up to the referee. "That's a penalty kick! That's a PK! You missed the call! That's the game right there!" The referee pretended not to hear. Two minutes later, with the ball caroming wildly in front of Norway's goal again, the referee blew her whistle. She signaled that Espeseth had committed a foul, a **hand ball.** This time Team USA received its penalty kick.

The crowd rose to its feet as the ball was placed 12 yards from the goal mouth. Michelle Akers would take the penalty kick. Norwegian goalkeeper Bente Nordby got set in a crouch. Akers came forward and gave the ball a terrific thump. Nordby dived for it. The ball shot past her into the right corner for a goal. As the crowd roared, Akers jumped for joy. Julie caught her in midair and bear hugged her. Their teammates poured onto the field to celebrate. The Americans had tied the game.

This was the first time women's soccer had ever been a part of the Olympic Games. "Becoming part of the Olympics is a breakthrough for girls' sports," Julie said. "Just to be a member of the first U.S. team makes me very proud. And then, to actually have a chance to win it . . ."

Julie is an important member of Team USA. She and Carla Overbeck are cocaptains of the team. As a **midfielder,** Julie creates plays and distributes the ball. Like a drummer in a rock 'n' roll band, she sets the rhythm and her teammates follow the beat. Coach Tony DiCicco says the players who score goals get the headlines in the newspapers, but soccer fans know who is the real star of Team USA. "Our opponents around the world try to stop our engine," he says. "That's Julie. She sees where the weakness of the other team is and goes for it. Or she sees where the strength of our team is and goes for it."

Neither team scored again in the second half. After 90 minutes of regulation play, Norway and Team USA were locked in a 1–1 tie. They would have to play a sudden-death overtime. The first team to score would win. The winning goal in overtime is known internationally as the "golden goal." This time, that name truly fit because the winning team would get to play three days later for the gold medal.

As the crowd stamped its feet and screamed for the Americans, the teams gathered at opposite sides of the field to plan for overtime. About 40 rows up from the field, amid a sea of red, white, and blue, nearly

40 of Julie's relatives and friends waved a huge banner they had made from a bedsheet. On it was written ROWDY FOUDY. "Everyone was crying and carrying on," said Julie's mother, Judy Foudy. "You shouldn't place so much emphasis on winning, but we couldn't help it."

Julie's family and friends made a banner to show support.

On the Team USA sideline, players were stretched out on the grass as team trainers massaged their legs. Julie stood among them and said, "This is our time! This is when they are going to lose! This is when we take it to 'em!" Julie remembered how Norway had broken their hearts a year earlier in the 1995 Women's World Cup semifinal. She remembered how the Norwegians had celebrated on the field with a silly human-centipede dance. "We aren't going to let that happen this time!" Julie announced. "They are not going to do that to us again!"

The referee called the teams back onto the field for the overtime period. The buzz of the crowd grew louder. Julie stood near the midfield stripe in her sweat-soaked jersey No. 11. She had chosen that number in sixth grade, when she was 11 years old, and she had worn it ever since. "It became my lucky number right away," she said. "I figured it meant I was double No. 1." Hege Riise, Norway's slick midfielder and one of the world's best players, lined up near Julie to mark her.

The Americans attacked at once. Under Julie's direction, they kept the ball in Norway's end of the field. Julie's pace seemed to quicken. She moved forward, pushing the ball and her teammates toward Norway's goal. The Norwegian defense stretched like a rubber band as it tried to hold back the American rush. Tall Norwegian Heide Stoere joined in trying to close down Julie. Several times the Norwegians managed to clear out the ball, but each time the Americans returned with it. Amid the chants of "U-S-A . . . U-S-A," Julie refused to let her team lose. "There's something I call 'The Rage,'" Julie explained. "It's a zone I go into sometimes. It's like I'm almost possessed on the field. When I'm there, I just won't lose."

Nine minutes into Team USA's relentless pounding in overtime, the Norwegians wilted. Julie took the ball at the center line and moved it up the right side. She cut inside past a defender to give herself more space. She dribbled toward the goal, waiting for a teammate to break free. She kept the ball near her feet by tap-tap-tapping it like a yo-yo on a string—waiting, waiting. Then she saw Shannon MacMillan run toward the goal. Just then Norway's left **centerback** raced at Julie. Julie thought, *If I can put the right pace on this ball, we win!* She kicked it behind the centerback and the ball threaded along the ground past another defender. MacMillan and Norway goalkeeper Nordby closed in on it but MacMillan got there first. She blasted the ball left and low. It whistled past Nordby and into the net.

Roars of joy filled the stadium as the American players dove to the ground in a celebration they call "The Slide." Julie was at the bottom of the pile. Then they were up on their feet screaming and running around the field with their arms in the air.

The 1996 Olympic Games were the first to include women's soccer as a medal sport.

Fans waved flags and the stadium lit up with hundreds of camera flashes. Julie's family and friends worked their way down through the crowd. Julie met them at the railing. "Everyone was hugging and going crazy," she said. "My brother Mike had tears coming down his face. Everyone was exhausted from screaming the whole game. They looked more worn out than me."

From an early age, Julie loved to play sports.

2

At Work and Play

Julie says her childhood was one long smile. "My parents let me be anything I wanted to be," she said. "They weren't the type to push me into soccer or sports or make me sit down and study. They've always just been there to support me."

Jim and Judy Foudy, Julie's parents, had met at an officers' party in Tacoma, Washington. Jim was a first lieutenant in the U.S. Army. Judy was studying to be a nurse. They dated for three years and then were married. A year later, they moved to Northern California and had a son named Michael. A year after that, a second son named Jeffrey was born. Three years later they had a daughter named Kristin. The Foudys moved to Southern California to raise their family. Four years later, on January 23, 1971, their second daughter and last child was born. They named her Julie.

Julie stands in front of her brothers and sister, from left, Michael, Kristin and Jeffrey.

Julie grew up in Mission Viejo, a quiet community at the edge of the Pacific Ocean. She lived in a beige two-story house on Minoa Drive, where she shared a bedroom with her sister, Kristin. Their room was wallpapered with bright yellow flowers and had twin beds with bright yellow bedspreads. Julie covered the wallpaper on her side of the room with sports posters.

"Kristin and I used to fight like cats," Julie said. "For instance, I was very fidgety and always moving in bed. The lights would be out and Kristin would say, 'If you don't stop moving, I'm going to let you have it.' And I'd accidentally move and she'd warn me, 'If you move one more time, that's it.' And I could feel an itch under my arm or somewhere. The itch would get worse and worse. I just had to scratch it. So I did. And she'd come over and punch me or throw pillows at me."

When Julie took her adventurous spirit outdoors, she sometimes frightened her mother half to death. At age three, Julie was popping wheelies on her Big Wheel and careening down the hill in front of the house. A year later she was skateboarding down the hill with pigtails on either side of her head flying in the air. Soon after, she was diving into the backyard pool from the wooden patio roof a story high. When her parents objected, she claimed she was forced to leap from there because the pool had no diving board. "She was very active and coordinated," said Judy Foudy, "and when she got hurt she didn't cry much. We have videos of her getting hit in the face with a ball, crying for just a moment, and then joining the game again. Somehow she never had to go to the emergency room."

Julie was a curious child who sometimes got into trouble. Once when she was four, she went into her brother's room with her next-door neighbor, Dougie Hall. Together they opened a cage door and released a dozen pet hamsters. Julie tried to capture the hamsters but she squeezed too hard and accidentally killed two of them. She did not play with the hamsters after that.

For her kindergarten school play, Julie was chosen to be Miss Muffet. Her teacher called to tell Judy that her daughter should wear a dress to school for the play. "Oh, she'll definitely wear a dress," Julie's mother assured her. But Julie threw a terrible fit. "I guess she figured her whole image would have been ruined," Judy said. That year Miss Muffet appeared in blue jeans.

Julie liked sports at an early age. She would sit with her father and brothers and watch Lakers and Dodgers games on television. "Women's sports weren't on TV back then, maybe a little tennis, but not much else," Julie said. "There certainly weren't any women soccer players on TV. My role models were people like Kareem Abdul-Jabbar, a 7-foot man I could never be like."

If a game was being played somewhere in the neighborhood, Julie was usually in the middle of it. She played basketball on her neighbors' driveways and tackle football at the elementary school's field.

Baseball was just one of the many sports Julie enjoyed playing.

She pitched and played catcher on Bobby Sox baseball teams her father coached. Her brothers surfed in the ocean, and Julie rode the waves alongside them on her little **boogie board.** Her sister played tennis, so Julie entered a tennis tournament. She finished last and was too embarrassed to try that sport again.

Julie's favorite sport was soccer. By first grade, she was so skilled at dribbling the ball with her feet that boys in the older grades would invite her to join them in games at recess and lunch. She begged her mother to sign her up in the American Youth Soccer Organization (AYSO), and her mother explained that six-year-olds were too young to join. She would have to wait a year. When Julie turned seven, her mother paid the $25 membership fee. Julie was an official member of AYSO Region 84.

The 1979 Soccerettes team was Julie's first traveling team. She is in the back row, third from the left.

Julie made the All-Star team as a midfielder her first year. Later she was recruited to play for a traveling club team called the Soccerettes. Julie picked jersey No. 8 because that was her age. When she found out the rest of the girls on the team were nine, she insisted she was that old, too. "But aren't you in second grade?" they would ask. "No, no," Julie fibbed, "I'm in third grade, just like you."

In second and third grade, Julie also sang in the school choir. The girls wore white blouses and skirts for performances. Not Julie. She wore shorts and a white shirt.

"I wanted to be a boy," Julie said. "I acted like a boy. I played tackle football with the boys at school. My brother's friends used to call me 'Jimmy.'"

Julie's favorite subjects at Del Cerro Elementary School were writing, science, and math. In Mrs. Amsted's third-grade class, the students' math scores were listed each day on the overhead projector. "I was always number two behind this girl named Helen," Julie said. "It just drove me crazy. One day I finally caught up with her. We ended the year tied."

Julie's soccer team traveled all around Southern California to play other teams. Julie played attacking midfielder and often led the team in scoring. Coach Jim Hutchinson took the Soccerettes to weekend tournaments in Northern California and sometimes took them out of the state.

Julie's Soccerettes team played in Norway one season.

The summer after seventh grade, Julie was lucky enough to go with the team to Norway to play in the Oslo Cup. Julie marveled at Europe's magnificent buildings, but she was more impressed with the candy bars. "I fell in love with Daim Bars," she said. "I was a candy freak."

By this time, Julie had fallen in love with soccer. She practiced at home by kicking the ball at the garage door. Eventually, the garage door had to be replaced. Inside the house, Julie lightly kicked the ball in the living room against a flat marble step a few inches high at the base of the fireplace. She had to keep the ball low to hit the side of the step. Her mother's expensive glass vase sat up on the step, but Julie never moved it. She thought it was a challenge to keep the ball low and not hit the vase.

"Julie, you're going to break my vase!" her mother often warned her.

"No, I won't," Julie said as she tapped the ball against the step.

"But what if you miss?"

"Don't worry, Mom. I won't miss."

One day Julie missed. She broke the vase. "I got a good earful," said Julie. "My mom was plenty mad."

Skiing was another sport Julie enjoyed as a youngster.

By the time she was in the eighth grade, Julie was an experienced soccer player.

3

Shooting Star

In the summer of 1984, when Julie was 13, the Olympic Games were held in Los Angeles. Patriotic fervor swept through Southern California as the area prepared to host the best athletes in the world. One day at Soccerettes practice, Coach Hutchinson told the girls that they were all invited to try out for a district team in the Olympic Development Program (ODP). The coach didn't know much more about the team. Julie and some of her teammates decided to go to the tryout. The team turned out to be for players 16 years and younger. Julie was the youngest girl to make the team.

Julie continued to play for the Soccerettes but she also played in the Olympic Development Program. She figured it was another league and another chance to play against good competition. But since women's soccer wasn't even included in the Olympics, she wondered why it was called an Olympic Development Program.

Julie joined the Mission Viejo High School soccer team as a freshman in 1985. A year later, she was named Player of the Year for Southern California the first of three times. She also was an all-league volleyball player and competed on the track team. For fun, she hung out at Aliso Beach with friends Heather McIntyre, Kerri Kennedy, and Stephanie and Kristi Burruel.

In high school, Julie played volleyball in addition to soccer.

The day Julie turned 16, she got her driver's license and her sister's hand-me-down red Volkswagen Beetle. Julie got a job at a snack place on the pier at the beach, but it turned out to be more play than work. "I would just sit there and invent these wild shakes and crazy brownies topped with everything," she said. "I ate up a storm." When it was time for work and responsibility, Julie grew intense and businesslike. She concentrated in class. At home, Julie often stayed up late to work on extra credit assignments. She studied at the big dining room table where she could spread out her books and notes and work in better lighting. "She was so disciplined," her mother said. "We never had to tell her to study. She just seemed to understand the value of an education."

The summer of 1987, Julie's local district team played several games against other districts in the area, just as they had the summers before. This time, though, a California team was selected from all the district teams to play against other western states. Julie was picked to play on the California team. It was a 19-and-under team, and 16-year-old Julie was among the youngest players.

To her surprise, within a month she was promoted again, this time to the West Regional team of 40 players. Taking a week's worth of clothes and money, she went to eastern Washington to play a few games against the teams from other regions of the country.

She played well again and was ready to return home when she was told she was among 18 girls selected to travel to Michigan for still more games. She called home. "Mom," she said, "can you send more money? I don't know what's going on, but I have to go to Michigan."

Northern Michigan University in the town of Marquette hosted the competition. Julie played a series of games, against mostly older girls. Olympic Development coaches were impressed with her skills and leadership. She moved gracefully with long strides and controlled the ball with either foot. She also was good at doing a **header.** Her field direction was sharp, and she carried a commanding presence.

When the competition ended, she was selected to play in yet another tournament, this time in Blaine, Minnesota. Julie was part of the national 19-and-under team. Mia Hamm, Kristine Lilly, and Joy Fawcett were also picked for her team. The United States women's national team would be there. So would teams from Sweden, Norway, Canada, and China.

In Minnesota, the U.S. women's national team lost in an early round. Julie's team won. Her youth team advanced to the championship game against Sweden. The Swedes won that game, but Julie impressed women's national team coach Anson Dorrance with her footwork and maturity. That night Julie called home again. "Mom! I need more money!" Julie told her parents.

"I'm going to China! With the U.S. women's national team! They just put me on the team!"

Julie enjoyed the trip to China, and she learned a lot. The team had scheduled two games in the northern Chinese cities of Tianjin and Shenyang. When the Americans arrived in Tianjin, Chinese people greeted them with wonder and amazement. "Most of them had never seen white people in person," said Julie. "They were coming up to us and touching our hair." Chinese officials declared the day of the game a town holiday and 76,000 people filled the stadium. The Americans defeated the Chinese team, 2–0. Ten days later in Shenyang, the teams battled to a 1–1 tie.

Julie did not play in either game but she practiced daily with her new teammates. "Balls were flying past me and people were flying past me," she said. "These women were good! I thought, 'What the heck am I doing out here?' Each day was a real confidence battle. And the games were worse. I'd always been a star, and here I was, sitting on the bench. Not that I wanted to go in the game. I was afraid to go in. I didn't want to mess up."

Julie returned to Southern California with a new perspective. "There was so much poverty in China," she said. "We were lucky just to get a warm shower. I came home appreciating all that we had here in America, all that I had taken for granted. I was thankful just to have water pour out of the faucet."

Julie's life became a whirlwind of soccer games. She practiced and played with the Soccerettes and with her high school team. She also trained with the women's national team and traveled to games in Japan, New Zealand, Canada, Australia, Taiwan, Sweden, Czechoslovakia, Norway, and West Germany. Through all the games with the national team, she sat on the bench. Substitutes are rarely used at this level of soccer because a player who comes out of a game cannot go back in.

On July 29, 1988, Julie finally got into her first international game, in Rimini, Italy. As she jogged onto the field, she thought, *Oh God, please don't let me mess up.* She played well, and Team USA beat France's national team, 1–0. "When the game ended, I wanted to keep playing," she said.

Back home, Julie's parents swelled with pride. "There was so much to brag about," Julie's mother said. "I'd be on the phone telling friends about Julie and she'd get really mad at me. She'd say, 'Mom, don't talk about me!' She was very humble."

In 1989, the Soccerettes team disbanded. Most of the other players had turned 19 and gone to college. Eighteen-year-old Julie had no club team on which to play. One day, she went to a sporting goods store to buy some soccer shoes. That's where she met Ian Sawyers. He was the store manager. He also coached a club team called the Nightmares.

Her high school soccer team was just one of three teams Julie played on as a teenager.

Julie remembered that the Soccerettes had played the Nightmares. Ian asked her in his thick English accent to join the Nightmares. "I loved his accent," said Julie, who joined his team that very day.

Julie starred for the Nightmares and led them to the national finals. Though by this time she had played in international competitions all over the world, Julie loved playing for the Nightmares. She had a big crush on Ian.

Julie and Ian began dating. Julie's parents became concerned that their daughter was too interested in Ian. They were afraid she would decide not to go to college and meet new people. Ian wanted to calm their fears. He asked to speak with them. Julie and her brother stood upstairs, leaning against the banister, one evening as Ian spoke to Judy and Jim in the living room. "I know you want Julie to go college," Ian told them. "I know you want her to meet new people. I want that for her, too. I am as proud of her as you are. Please believe me when I tell you that I am not going to be a chain around her neck." Julie and Jim felt relieved. They trusted Ian. "We were really impressed," Judy said.

During Julie's senior year in high school, her family moved into another house in nearby Laguna Niguel.

Julie's classmates elected her homecoming queen during her senior year at Mission Viejo High School.

As Julie was packing her belongings, she came across a journal she had written in fourth grade. Julie had named her journal "Bertha." In the journal, she had written an entry that read:

Dear Bertha,
Mrs. Miller wants us to make a New Year's Resolution. My New Year's resolution is two things.
1) Stop chewing my fingernails.
2) Get straight A's so I can go to Stanford.
Sincerely, Julie

Julie had received more than a hundred letters from schools offering her a soccer **scholarship.** Monday nights were "recruiting night" when coaches called. Julie's phone never stopped ringing. Eventually she narrowed her choices to four universities—Harvard, North Carolina, Stanford, and California-Berkeley. Then she whittled it down to two—North Carolina and Stanford. Anson Dorrance, the national women's team coach, was also the coach at North Carolina. Julie liked Coach Dorrance. Several members of the national team played at North Carolina, so it seemed a good place for Julie. But for a long time she had dreamed of attending Stanford. The problem was, Stanford cost $20,000 a year but the school offered Julie only a partial scholarship, about $2,000 a year. Where would Julie get the rest of the money? North

Carolina cost much less. When Coach Dorrance met with Julie's parents one night for dinner, he said, "How would you like us to save you $80,000?"

But in the end, Julie chose Stanford. Her parents borrowed money from the bank to pay for classes and books. "We were proud of Julie," her mother said. "We were pleased that she was thinking about her future academically." Once Julie had made her decision, she dreaded telling Coach Dorrance the news. She did not want to hurt his feelings. She cringed whenever the phone rang. When they finally did speak, the coach told Julie how glad he was to have her on the national team.

Julie's high school years ended with the senior prom and a week of festivities at places like Knott's Berry Farm and Disneyland in the early summer of 1989. Julie missed all of it. She even missed her graduation ceremony. While her friends were receiving their diplomas and then flying to Mazatlan, Mexico, for a celebration, Julie was in Colorado training with the national team. "The decision to be with the team was mine," she said. "My parents supported me either way. They said 'Go with what your heart is telling you.' Well, the night of my graduation, I was heartsick. I talked to Kristine Lilly about it. She was the homesick type and she could relate to me. I questioned myself and whether I should have come to Colorado. I felt like I was missing out on so much."

Judy and Jim Foudy were proud of their daughter Julie.

As if by magic, Coach Dorrance came to Julie with wonderful news the night of her graduation. He was promoting her to the first team. She had won a starting spot in the midfield. "All at once," said Julie, "I felt like I had made the right decision."

She flew to Italy with her teammates for a game against Poland and played every minute of a 0–0 tie. She returned with them to Colorado and then flew on to Los Angeles with a smile on her face. She met her parents at the airport, gave them each a big hug, and boarded the next flight for Mazatlan. There, her high school friends were waiting.

Julie earned Freshman of the Year honors at Stanford.

4

All around the World

College life was just what Julie had thought it would be—part fun and games, part work and responsibility. Besides dating Ian, who visited about once a month, Julie made many new friends. But she also had three main responsibilities: 1) Play soccer for Stanford, 2) Play soccer for the national team, and 3) Study. She managed these responsibilities with the balance of a tightrope walker.

Julie had a "fan club" for her games at Stanford's Maloney Field. Many of her relatives—aunts, uncles, cousins, and grandparents—lived near the Northern California campus. They often came to see her play. Grams rode with Aunt Bobbie and Uncle Bob. Uncle Mike and Aunt Julie brought cousins Jeffrey, Patrick, and Christopher. Back home, Julie's mother often worked weekends as a nurse, but she and Julie's dad would come when they could. Ian sometimes came, too.

Stanford went to the NCAA soccer tournament all four years Julie played for the Cardinal.

They all sat as close to the field as they could. Aunt Bobbie and Uncle Bob sometimes had the entire Stanford team—the coaches and all 24 players—over to their house for a big pancake breakfast. Uncle Bob was the master of the apple cinnamon pancake.

Julie was a superstar for Stanford. Playing attacking midfielder, she led the Cardinal to the National Collegiate Athletic Association Tournament all four years. As a freshman, she was the team's Most Valuable Player and was named NCAA Freshman of the Year.

Her next three years, she was first-team All-America. After her junior year, Julie was chosen as the Player of the Year by *Soccer America.* She finished her career as the Cardinal's all-time leader in goals and assists. When she wasn't zigzagging through opponents on Maloney Field, she was helping at camps for girls, teaching them some of her skills and secrets.

Julie became a leader on the U.S. national team, too. In 1991, she played in 24 games against international competition, scoring five goals and 10 assists, as Team USA lost just five times. She encouraged young players who joined the team, telling them to stay confident even when they doubted themselves. Once, on the way to a game, newcomer Tiffeny Milbrett confided to Julie that she did not think she was good enough to be on the team. Julie had a long talk with Tiffeny, assuring her that feeling that way was normal. "It wasn't long ago that I went through just what you're feeling," Julie whispered. "Just keep convincing yourself that you belong. If you let it overcome you, you're done. Keep telling yourself, 'I belong here.' One day you'll realize it's true."

Since 1930, the biggest competition in men's soccer has been the World Cup. Like football's Super Bowl or baseball's World Series, the World Cup involves the best teams. The Federation Internationale de Football Association (FIFA), soccer's world governing body, runs the tournament. (Soccer is called "football" everywhere but in North America.) Eventually, FIFA organizers realized that women should be included, too. In 1991, FIFA staged the first Women's World Cup. The two-week tournament was played in China.

A few weeks before the event began, Julie told her parents, "This is the World Cup! Do you understand what that means?"

"No," they said.

"It's huge! It's gigantic! You need to come."

"Really? All the way to China?"

Julie's parents went, as did most of the other players' families. The Americans saw a country awash with festivities. Banners hung from trees and lampposts. Enormous floral statues lined the streets. Soccer merchandise was everywhere. The games were broadcast on nearly every TV station in China. The parents of the American team stayed together in a hotel and visited sites like the Great Wall. And, of course, they attended the games.

Team USA beat Sweden, Brazil, Japan, Taiwan, Germany, and, finally, Norway. Julie played every minute of every game. The final against Norway was played at Tianhe Stadium in the sprawling southern China city of Guangzhou. Before a crowd of 65,000, each team scored a goal in the first half. The game stayed tied until the dying moments. With barely two minutes left in the 90-minute contest, midfielder Michelle Akers stole a pass and pushed the ball past the Norwegian goalkeeper to win it. Afterward, beneath a huge shower of fireworks, Julie and her teammates received their championship medals and huge bouquets of flowers. Their parents cheered from the stands and waved tiny American flags.

Women's soccer was not yet popular in the United States, but Julie flew home expecting the great international victory to propel her sport into the spotlight. That did not happen. "No one was at the airport to greet us," Julie said. "You'd think that maybe five newspapers would have noticed what we did. I really felt let down. It was like, we got so much out of it personally, but we had no one to share it with. We thought winning the first World Cup was a huge leap for our sport, but it was only a baby step."

Being on the road so much meant Julie had to work extra hard to keep up with her college studies. She read her course books on buses and airplanes. Friends sent her their class notes. Professors faxed her the quizzes and tests. She took midterm tests in her hotel room under the supervision of national team administrator Heather Kashner. Between games at the World Cup, Julie locked herself in her room and studied for final exams. When she returned from China and showed up at her first class the next day, her professor said, "You won the World Cup? Oh. That's wonderful. Welcome back. Here is your final exam in human biology."

Two years later, Julie completed her degree. While her national team played a match against Team Canada in June 1993, Julie was back at Stanford, dressed in cap and gown, receiving her diploma. "I already missed my high school graduation," she said. "There's no way I was going to miss my other one."

A year later, Julie scored high marks on a series of difficult tests and was accepted by Stanford Medical School. Her plan was to become a doctor. But then something came up—the 1995 World Cup. Julie was cocaptain of the national team, and she was eager to help her team defend its 1991 title. Her team had a new coach. Tony DiCicco replaced Anson Dorrance, who had retired a year earlier. Julie asked Stanford administrators to allow her to start medical school a year later, and they agreed.

The 1995 World Cup was played in Sweden, and this time Julie's sister and brothers joined her parents on the trip. They watched Julie's team tie China and then defeat Denmark, Australia, and Japan to reach the semifinal game. Julie had scored the tournament's most inspiring goal, a header against Australia, to tie that game and spur the team to victory.

But in the semifinal, the Americans could not muster a goal. Norway's Ann Kristin Aarones scored 10 minutes into the game to take a 1–0 lead. At halftime Julie said, "C'mon you guys, let's get our act together! They're killing us out there!" Team USA pushed the attack in the second half but couldn't finish. Each time the ball neared Norway's goal, it was cleared away. As time ticked away, the Americans grew nervous and tight. They misplayed balls, lost their rhythm, and soon lost the game.

When the final whistle sounded, Julie collapsed on the field, exhausted and embarrassed. She and her teammates sat and watched the Norwegians celebrate by forming a chain and crawling on their knees like a centipede. "I was disgusted with myself," said Julie. "Toward the end of the game, when the team really needed me, I should have kicked it into high gear, but instead I was drained of energy and could hardly finish. What kind of shape was I in to let that happen? I felt like I had failed, I had let the team down.

After losing in the 1995 World Cup semifinals, the U. S. team vowed to do better.

Julie and Ian are all smiles after their wedding.

I made a promise to myself that I would never let that happen again, ever! Then the whole team gathered right there on the field and made a vow that if we ever got in this position again, we would win!"

Julie's spirits were much higher a month later. On July 30, 1995, she and Ian were married. Julie's friends and teachers from high school and college attended the wedding, as did Ian's family from

England. The national team was playing a game in Connecticut that day against Chinese Taipei, but midfielder Kristine Lilly and **forward** Karen Gabarra skipped the game and flew to Southern California to attend. Defender Joy Fawcett had a broken foot so she, too, was able to be there. Her daughter, Katelyn, was the flower girl.

Julie wore a white wedding gown with her hair pulled up in the front and down in back. After the reception, Julie and Ian left on their honeymoon to Hawaii. On the final day of their trip, the national team played rival Norway in the final of a tournament. Julie watched the game on a television at the Maui airport. Team USA won, 2–0. "It killed me not to be there," said Julie. "But then again, I was having fun being with Ian."

Later that year, Julie heard some disturbing news. A television news report said that large American sporting goods companies were hiring workers in poor countries to make soccer balls. Foreign workers would work for less money than Americans. An undercover investigation showed that children as young as 9 or 10 years old were being forced by their families to work all day. Stitching a soccer ball by hand takes four hours, 32 polyester panels, and 642 stitches. Children often had to make three or four balls a day, stitching until their fingers bled.

This news bothered Julie. She cared deeply about

children and wished there were something she could do to help. Julie was already busy working with the U.S. government on an antismoking campaign in which she visited elementary schools and appeared in posters.

In April 1996, Julie and cocaptain Carla Overbeck went to the White House to meet with Donna Shalala, the Secretary of Health and Human Services, about the anti-smoking campaign. After lunch in the mess hall, Shalala said, "I have a half hour before my next meeting. Do you guys want a tour? Let's go up to the Oval Office." Shalala led Julie and Carla down the back halls of the White House. Arriving at the Oval Office door, Shalala asked a Secret Service agent if the President was in the room. "Actually, he is," said the agent.

"Oh well," said Shalala, "we can't show you the room if he's in there. C'mon, let's go down to the Cabinet Room." Together they walked down a hallway, turned a corner, and Julie bumped smack into President Bill Clinton. "Hey!" Julie said. "We were just looking for you!" Shalala introduced the President to Julie and Carla. "Happy to meet you both," he said. "It's very nice of you to volunteer your time for the antismoking campaign. Thanks for coming out and helping us with this." The President chatted with the women for a couple of minutes, and afterward Julie was thrilled. "He was real nice. Just a regular guy," she said. "Carla and I had a blast."

Julie met President Bill Clinton at the White House.

A month later, the Chicago Bulls won the National Basketball Association championship. Star player Michael Jordan, who made millions of dollars from sporting goods companies, was asked in front of hundreds of reporters his opinion about **endorsing** shoes and balls that were made in other countries with child labor. Jordan would not answer. In the weeks that followed, he was asked the same question several more times. Each time, he had nothing to say. This silence disturbed Julie. "I am very concerned about the attitude of other professional athletes," she said. "I would hope that they would begin to care and speak up."

Winning an Olympic gold medal thrilled Julie.

5

Heart of Gold

Julie was planning to start medical school in the fall of 1996. But as the time drew near, she began thinking about the Olympic Games. Women's soccer was going to be included in the Olympics for the first time. Julie didn't want to miss the chance to play for a gold medal. She asked Stanford officials if she could delay her studies again. School officials didn't want to lose her permanently so they told her she could wait yet another year.

The Olympics opened with Julie's team beating Denmark, 3–0, and Sweden, 2–1. Then a scoreless tie against China enabled Team USA to advance to the semifinal round for a showdown with Norway. In that game's 18th minute, Norway's Agnete Carlsen intercepted a ball and passed it to Linda Medalen. Medalen slid it past U.S. goalkeeper Briana Scurry for a goal. Julie's team did not panic. After its World Cup loss to Norway, the team had hired sports psychologist Colleen Hacker to teach the players the mental side of the game. "We learned if we trailed in a game [we should] stay calm," said Julie. "We learned to believe in ourselves, that somehow we would win, instead of feeling like the floor was dropping out." The Americans won in overtime, 2–1.

Julie's team played China in the gold medal game. On a warm Georgia evening, 76,489 people filled Sanford Stadium in Athens. It was the largest crowd ever to watch a women's athletic event in any sport! Fans saw the Americans score in the 18th minute when Mia Hamm's shot bounced off the left post and Shannon MacMillan hammered home the **rebound.** China answered in the 32nd minute when Sun Wen stole a pass and chipped the ball into the net.

With the score tied 1–1, Julie and her teammates struggled to keep up with the swift Chinese, who continued to press the attack to halftime. "We didn't panic," said Julie. "There was a calm in the locker room. We said, 'OK, they outplayed us in the first half. But the second half is ours.' We knew we would have that gold medal around our necks."

The Americans struck gold in the 68th minute. Joy Fawcett raced down the right side and passed the ball to Tiffeny Milbrett, who rammed home the winning goal. "Then we just burned away the rest of the clock by playing keep-away," Julie said.

Julie avoids a defender during the gold medal game.

The final whistle touched off an explosion of cheers all around the stadium. The U.S. players went crazy. Julie and Mia Hamm screamed into a video camera, "That's right! That's what we've been training for!" Afterward Julie told reporters, "This was all that I had dreamed and a hundred times better. I want to remember this feeling every day."

Upon returning to Los Angeles with her family, Julie was met at the airport by a mass of people. She removed her gold medal from her backpack and passed it around the crowd. "People wanted to feel it and hold it," Julie's mother said. "Strangers would come up with little kids and say, 'Oh, put it on my daughter.'" At home, Julie loaned the medal to a neighbor to use at a police fundraiser. "You trust me with it?" said the neighbor. "Hey," Julie said, "you're a sheriff. It's safer with you than with anybody." When Ian's parents left town after a visit, they left behind a roll of film on the kitchen counter. Julie and Ian developed the film and found photographs of his parents in all different rooms of the house posing with the medal. After Julie showed a Federal Express delivery driver the medal, the regular mail carrier knocked at the door a bit later and said, "Is it true there's a gold medal here?" An hour later the UPS delivery driver knocked and said, "I hear there's an Olympic medal at this house. . . ."

Julie had become a role model for girls. She received letters and emails from fans across the country. One young New York girl wrote: "I hope this is Julie Foudy the soccer player. You are my hero. Finally I have a role model. If it wasn't for you I'd probably have to play golf. I hate golf." Julie made visits to schools around the country with her medal and a message that there is a time for play and a time for work. "The kids' reaction to the Olympics is what shocked me the most," she said. "We really weren't on TV all that much, but they seem to know everything about us."

Then Julie made another visit. It was to a poor village on the other side of the world. There was something Julie wanted to see there. Reebok company officials asked Julie to endorse their soccer ball. Before agreeing, she first wanted to travel to Pakistan to see for herself how the ball was made. "It was very unusual for an athlete to do this," said Reebok official Matt Lamcor. "Athletes are happy to endorse products because they get paid well for it. But Julie was extremely adamant about being involved and making this a personal issue." Julie explained her concern by saying, "If I was going to be a spokesperson for the ball, I wanted to be educated. I wanted to see with my own eyes how the balls are made, rather than hear about it from a million miles away."

Julie flew with several Reebok officials to Singapore, then to Karachi, Pakistan, then to Lahore. From there, she drove two hours on a small dirt road past donkeys and goats to the town of Sialkot at the foot of the Himalayas. Most of the world's soccer balls are made there. "Through the windows of the homes I saw people inside stitching soccer balls by hand," she said. "I learned their wage was about seven cents an hour."

Her athletic skills and friendly personality make Julie a favorite with soccer fans.

Child labor takes place in the children's homes. Raw materials for the soccer balls are dropped off at various homes each morning. The stitched balls are gathered up at day's end. "Everyone knew that children were doing some of the stitching," said Julie. "Nine-and 10-year-olds were working for pennies an hour. They were stitching balls they were never going to use. The families did it to survive and to keep the ball manufacturers happy with their tiny village's work."

Jim Foudy sports a Reebok cap after Julie agreed to endorse Reebok products. Julie asked the company to be fair to its workers.

Dozens of companies made soccer balls. Reebok was one of the few that promised not to hire children. The company built a huge factory where all their balls were made. Workers there had to be at least 15 years old. Julie toured the factory and spoke to the owners and employees. "I grilled them for hours about what was going on," she said. Reebok director Doug Cahn agreed. "She asked a lot of tough questions," he said. "It helped us be better aware of all the precautions we need to take."

Reebok stamped its balls with: "Guaranteed: Manufactured without child labor." After spending three days in Sialkot and the surrounding villages, Julie was satisfied the guarantee was true. She agreed to endorse Reebok's ball. Before she left, she walked through a tiny village carrying a few soccer balls. She saw children peeking over walls and around corners as she went by. She stood in the middle of a pasture and started waving and hollering, "C'mon over!" Then she began juggling a soccer ball with her feet. Suddenly she was surrounded by about 20 boys jumping up and down. Julie showed them juggling on the head and thighs and feet. Soon all the boys were laughing and taking turns trying to juggle. A few girls stood to one side. Julie called them over, but they preferred to watch. "These kids were dirt poor, but they had such a spirit to them," Julie said. "It was time for me to leave, and so I waved good-bye, and a little boy about four years old ran up and grabbed my hand and tried to keep me there. It broke my heart."

Julie's trip to Pakistan became national news. "I just wanted to try to do something to help," she said. "I had no idea it would be such a big deal to the media. All I know is, I'll never look at a ball the same way again."

A day later Julie was back with the national team in Australia for more international matches. Medical school was approaching, but she still wanted to represent her country playing soccer. "I've got to make a decision to do medical school or to do soccer," she told reporters. "In my heart, I still want to play soccer." Julie wrote a letter to Stanford. She thanked the school officials for being so patient with her and told them that she had finally decided not to attend medical school.

In early 1998, soccer's world governing body honored Julie with the prestigious Fair Play award. FIFA recognized her "commitment to bringing an end to the use of child labor in the manufacture of soccer balls." She was the first American to receive the award and also the first woman. But when Julie was told that she needed to fly to Paris, France, to be honored, she said she could not go. Her team was playing that day in China. "I need to help my team, so I'm not going," she said. International soccer officials insisted that she attend. Julie reluctantly agreed and traveled to Paris to be honored.

When Julie isn't busy playing with the national team, she likes to snowboard, in-line skate, golf, and coach at the Julie Foudy Soccer Camp. She also worked as a TV announcer for the 1998 Men's World Cup.

"I'm so excited for our sport," Julie says. "It's becoming more popular all the time. It's wild to see people so affected by it, especially kids, especially girls. We've gone from unknowns to getting cheers from strangers on the street. There's almost a frenzy wherever we go. Soccer is such a fun sport to play, and it's so healthy to play it. Any boy or girl who develops an interest in soccer is a lucky boy or girl. And how lucky I am, how truly lucky, to get to be a part of that."

Career Highlights

- Three-time Southern California Player of the Year, 1986-88
- Made first appearance with U.S. national team at age 17, Italy, July 29, 1988
- Named NCAA Freshman of the Year, 1989
- Three-time NCAA All-America selection, 1990-92
- Named Soccer America Player of the Year, 1991
- Member of U.S. national team that won Women's World Cup gold medal, China, 1991
- Stanford University's all-time leader in goals and assists, 1989-92
- Member of U.S. national team that won Women's World Cup bronze medal, Sweden, 1995
- Member of U.S. national team that won Olympic gold medal, Atlanta Games, 1996
- First woman and first American to receive FIFA Fair Play award, 1998

Julie and Ian show off the gold!

Glossary

boogie board: A short surfboard.

centerback: One of the players, called fullbacks, who play nearest his or her own goalkeeper. The centerback is the fullback who plays in the middle of the field.

endorsing: Encouraging others to buy a certain product in return for money from the company that makes the product.

forward: One of the players whose primary purpose is to score goals.

goalkeeper: The player who guards his or her team's own goal.

hand ball: The foul that is called when a player plays the ball with a hand or any part of the arm beyond the shoulder. Only the goalkeeper is allowed to touch the ball with a hand or arm.

header: Hitting the ball with the forehead, near the hairline. The photo on the next page shows a player doing a header.

marking: Guarding an opponent.

midfielder: One of the players who play between the forwards and the fullbacks. A midfielder must play both defense and offense.

penalty kick: A free kick taken after a major violation is committed by the opponents in their

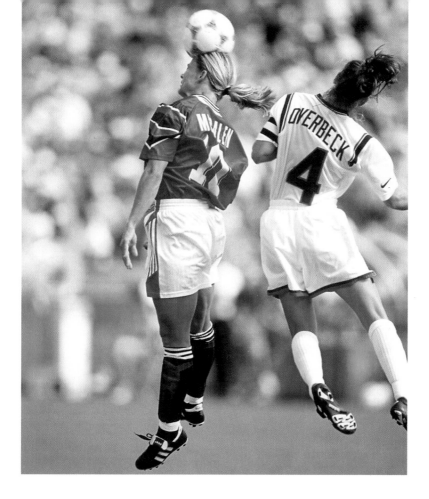

own penalty area. The kick is taken 12 yards in front of the center of the goal.

rebound: The bounce of the ball when it hits a goal post or the goalkeeper.

scholarship: Money a college or organization gives a student to pay for his or her education. Colleges often award scholarships to students who are outstanding scholars, athletes, musicians, or leaders.

Sources

Information from this book was obtained from the following sources: Interviews with Julie Foudy, Judy Foudy, Sue Rodin, Brian Remedi. Articles by: Tom Bonen (*Chicago Daily Southtown*, 4 May 1997); Gary Davidson (*USA Today*, 9 May 1997); Bonnie DeSimone (*Chicago Tribune*, 3 May 1997); Chris Dortch (*Chattanooga Times*, 28 October 1997); Dan Giesin (*San Francisco Chronicle*, 26 May 1997); Mike Jensen (*The Philadelphia Inquirer*, 5 June 1997); Jerry Langdon (*USA Today*, 9 January 1998); Ridge Mahoney (*Soccer Now*, Spring 1995); Gretchen McKay (*Pittsburgh Post-Gazette*, 5 November 1997); Spencer Patterson (*The Arizona Republic*, 6 August 1997); Scott Reid (*The Orange County Register*, 15 April 1996); Karen Rosen (*The Atlanta Journal-Constitution*, 23 July 1997); Carole Slezak (*Chicago Sun-Times*, 15 February 1998); Ben Smith III (*The Atlanta Journal-Constitution*, 29 July 1996); Jamie Trecker (*USA Today*, 29 July 1996, 2 August 1996); George Vecsey (*The New York Times*, 14 July 1996, 28 July 1996); Mark Whicker (*The Orange County Register*, 16 January 1998).

Further Reading

Coleman, Lori. *Fundamental Soccer.* Minneapolis: Lerner Publications Company, 1995.

Parker, David L. *Stolen Dreams, Portraits of Working Children.* Minneapolis: Lerner Publications Company, 1997.

Index

Write to Julie:

You can send mail to Julie at the address on the right. If you write a letter, don't get your hopes up too high. Julie and other athletes get lots of letters every day, and they aren't always able to answer them all.

Mrs. Julie Foudy
U.S. Soccer House
1801 South Prairie Avenue
Chicago, Il 60616

Acknowledgments

Photographs reproduced with permission of: SportsChrome East/ West, Rob Tringali, Jr., p. 1; © ALLSPORT USA/Andy Lyons, p. 2; © ALLSPORT USA/David Cannon, pp. 6, 61; Courtesy of the Foudy Family, pp. 10, 14, 16, 19, 20, 22, 23, 24, 26, 32, 35, 43, 44, 56, 59; © J. Brett Whitesell/ISI, pp. 13, 48, 51; © William Ing, p. 31; © Rod Searcey, pp. 36, 38; White House photo, p. 47; © Michael Allen, pp. 52, 55.

Front cover photograph by © ALLSPORT USA/Stephen Dunn.
Back cover photograph courtesy of Reebok.

Artwork by Lejla Fazlic Omerovic.

About the Author

Jeff Savage is the author of more than 30 sports books for young readers, including Lerner's *Tiger Woods*, *Grant Hill*, and *Eric Lindros*. A freelance writer, Jeff lives with his family in California.

B   Savage, Jeff,
FOU   1961-

       Julie Foudy.

$22.60   30061000003950

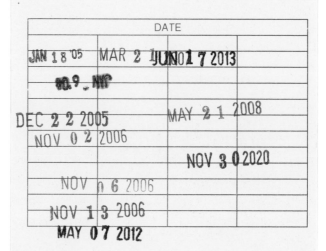

DATE			
JAN 18 '05	MAR 2	JUN 17 2013	
00.9 NP?			
DEC 2 2 2005		MAY 2 1 2008	
NOV 0 2 2006			
		NOV 3 0 2020	
NOV 0 6 2006			
NOV 1 3 2006			
MAY 0 7 2012			

000.